I ♥ love the farm
Giant Activity Book

D1450345

priddy books
big ideas for little people

What **FOOD** do we get from cows?

Butter

USE it to cover **TOAST** or **BREAD**, it's everybody's **FAVORITE** spread

milk

DO you like **COLD milk** before bed? or perhaps a **HOT** chocolate instead?

cream IS DELICIOUS poured on desserts!

mmm...cheese...

? HOW MANY different **cheeses** have you tried?

Learn to draw

Look at the picture and the word, then trace over the outlines.

COW

COW

Now draw the cow and fill in the letters to write its name.

1

C _ _

Follow the lines

Can you trace over the lines to lead the moms to their babies?

2

3

4

5

6

7

8

9

10

11

Moo maze

Can you find a way through the maze to lead the cow to her calf?

12

Start

Finish

13

Adding farm animals

Write the number of farm animals in the boxes, then add them up.

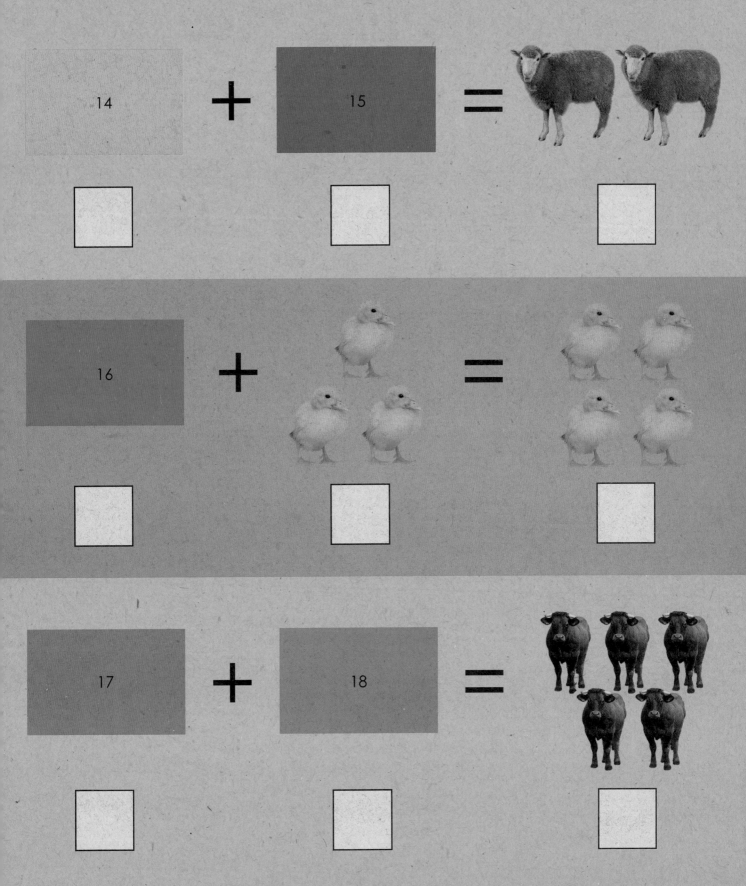

Counting farm animals

Count the farm animals and
write the totals in the boxes.

How many
pigs can
you count?

19

How many
horses can
you count?

20

How many
ducks can
you count?

How many
sheep can
you count?

How many
roosters can
you count?

How many
cows can
you count?

odd one out

Which farm animal is different from all the others?

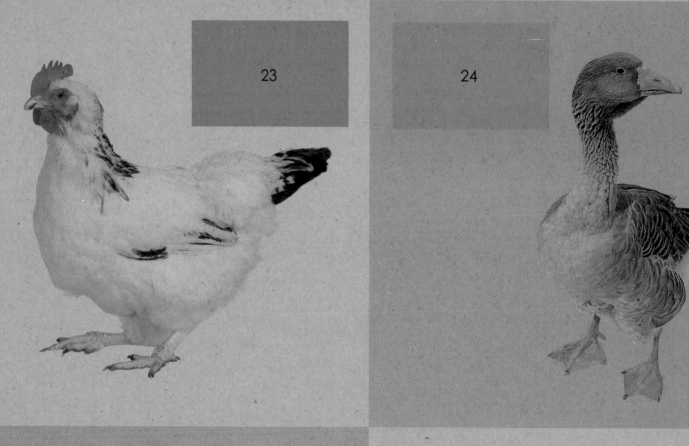

23

24

25

26

Missing halves

Can you draw the other halves of the pictures? Use the stickers to help you.

28

27

Turkey

The turkey is a funny **bird**, his **gobble** noise I'm sure you've **heard**

Drake

A male duck is called a DRAKE, he likes to hang out on the lake

Noisy bit

A group of geese is called a **GAGGLE**

ds

Chickens lay **eggs** that we love to eat, **SCRAMBLED** or fried - what a treat!

"Cock-a-doodle-doo" says the **rooster** in the MORNING, telling everyone that the day is DAWNING

Hungry chicks

Color in the chicks, then trace over their name.

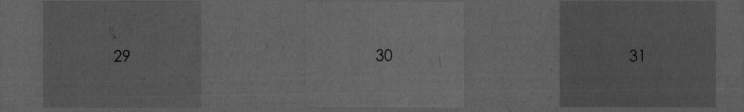

29   30   31

swimming duck

Color in the duck, then trace over its name.

Chicken scene

Can you make this chicken scene look really cute?
Look at the pictures below for ideas, add the
ones you like to the scene, then color it in!

tree

Add a tree to the background.

chicken coop

Chickens live in a coop.
Why not add one to the scene?

grass

Chickens like to walk
in the grass.

sunshine

Is it a sunny day on
the farm?

chick

Can you draw a
newly hatched chick?

Exactly the same

Only two roosters are exactly the same. Can you circle them?

How many?

Count the farm trucks and write the totals in the boxes.

38

39

40

41

On the pond

Color in the busy pond scene. How many animals can you count?

42   43   44

goose

gosling

45   46   47

dragonfly

duck

frog

"Come on, it's time to drink some milk"

"It's my turn next!"

Woolly
friends

In **SUMMERTIME** we **shear** their coats, but it doesn't hurt the **sheep** or **goats**

Llamas might look rather **SCRUFFY,** but their **coats** are soft and **FLUFFY!**

MALE goats are called **billy** GOATS

"Let's eat those flowers!"

Friendly goat

Color in the goat, then trace over its name.

48   49   50

Learn to draw

Look at the picture and the word, then trace over the outlines.

sheep

Now draw the sheep and fill in the letters to write its name.

51

S _ _ _ _

Coloring time

Color in the pictures, using the stickers to help you.

52

53

Farm words

Can you trace over the letters to complete the farm words?

54

horse

tractor

55

turkey

donkey

Dot to dots

Connect the dots to complete the pictures, then color them in.

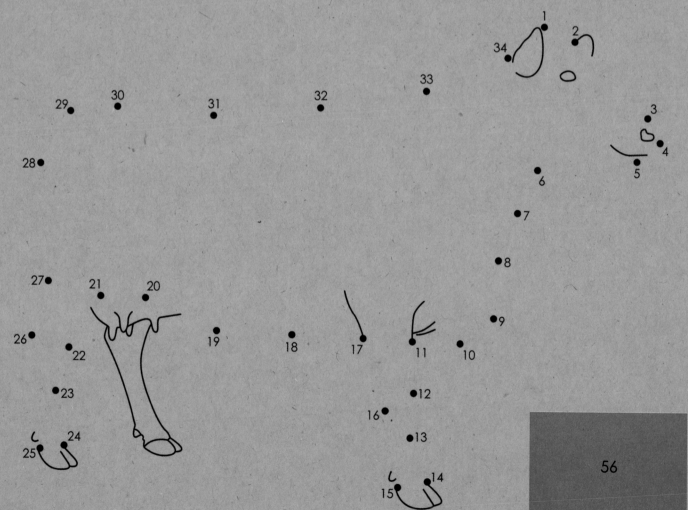

Big barn

Color in the barn, then trace over its name.

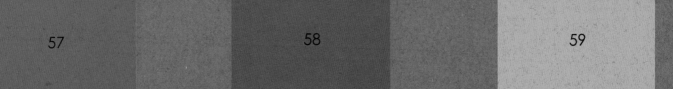

| 57 | 58 | 59 |

barn

Pink piglets are so very sweet,
they grow because they EAT and EAT

Perfect pigs

Rolling in MUD is great fun,
it helps pigs cool off in the hot sun!

Learn to draw

Look at the picture and the word, then trace over the outlines.

pig

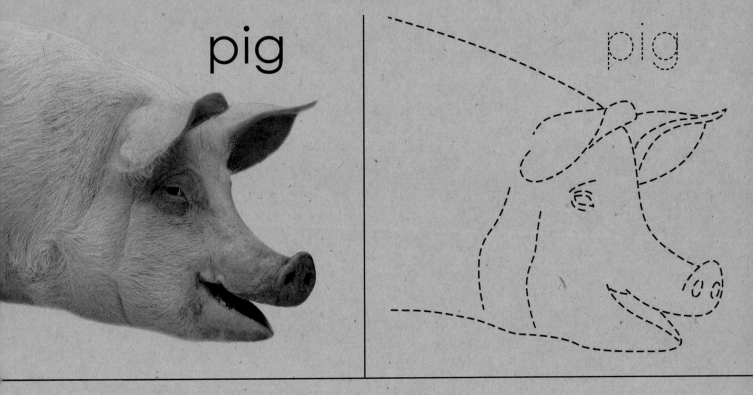

pig

Now draw the pig and fill in the letters to write its name.

p__

Matching letters

Draw a line between each animal and the letter its name begins with.

h

61

g

62

p

s

d

63

c

Fierce bull

Color in the bull, then trace over its name.

 64

 65

66

Pigs playing

Can you color in the pigs and make this scene really muddy?

67 68 69

Which pig is splashing and getting dirty in the mud?

Horse and foal

Color in the horse and foal, then trace over their names.

73	74	75

horse and foal

Noisy animals

Can you draw a line between each animal and the noise that it makes?

moo

76

cheep

naa

baa

77

neigh

oink

78

quack

79

Learn to draw

Look at the picture and the word, then trace over the outlines.

tractor

tractor

Now draw the tractor and fill in the letters to write its name.

t_ _ _ _ _ _

Word search

Can you find the farm words in the word search?

g	y	p	j	s	a	k	l	r	v
r	g	o	o	s	e	k	c	e	x
n	y	k	z	r	j	h	o	b	j
m	t	g	c	b	o	o	w	l	t
g	e	g	i	q	l	r	p	b	r
w	p	d	p	b	n	s	w	c	a
a	c	h	i	c	k	e	n	k	c
b	h	l	g	r	e	n	b	j	t
c	t	m	l	r	c	v	b	m	o
f	e	u	r	o	j	y	p	m	r

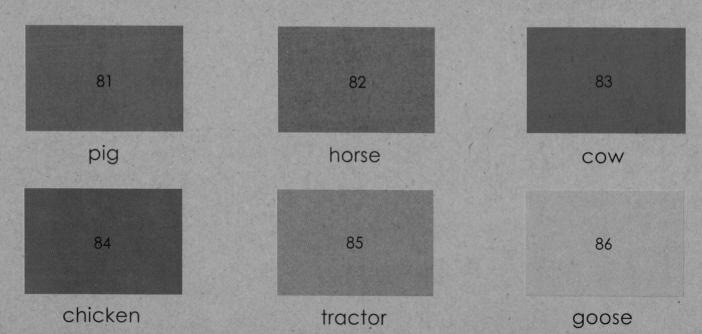

81

pig

82

horse

83

cow

84

chicken

85

tractor

86

goose

Shetland pony

Color in the shetland pony, then trace over its name.

87	88	89

shetland pony

This man's name is **Farmer BOB**, he's always **BUSY** with a **JOB**

The **VET** VISITS the **farm**, to check the animals **HAVEN'T** come to **HARM**

Friends

DONKEYS have huge **ears!**

Sheepdog
I help the farmer round up sheep in the **FIELDS**

"quack quack"

says the duck with her ducklings in line,
we must HURRY to get to the pond on time

and families

Cats

No farm is
complete without
some cats, they
run around and
catch the RATS!

Mix and match

Can you draw lines between the pairs of matching farm animals?

90

91

92

93

94

95

96

97

98

99

DOT to dot

Conect the dots to complete the picture, then color
it in using the colored dots as a guide.

In the field

Can you color the cows and sheep to make this scene really colorful?

100

101

102

What is a baby cow called? What is a baby sheep called?

103

104

105

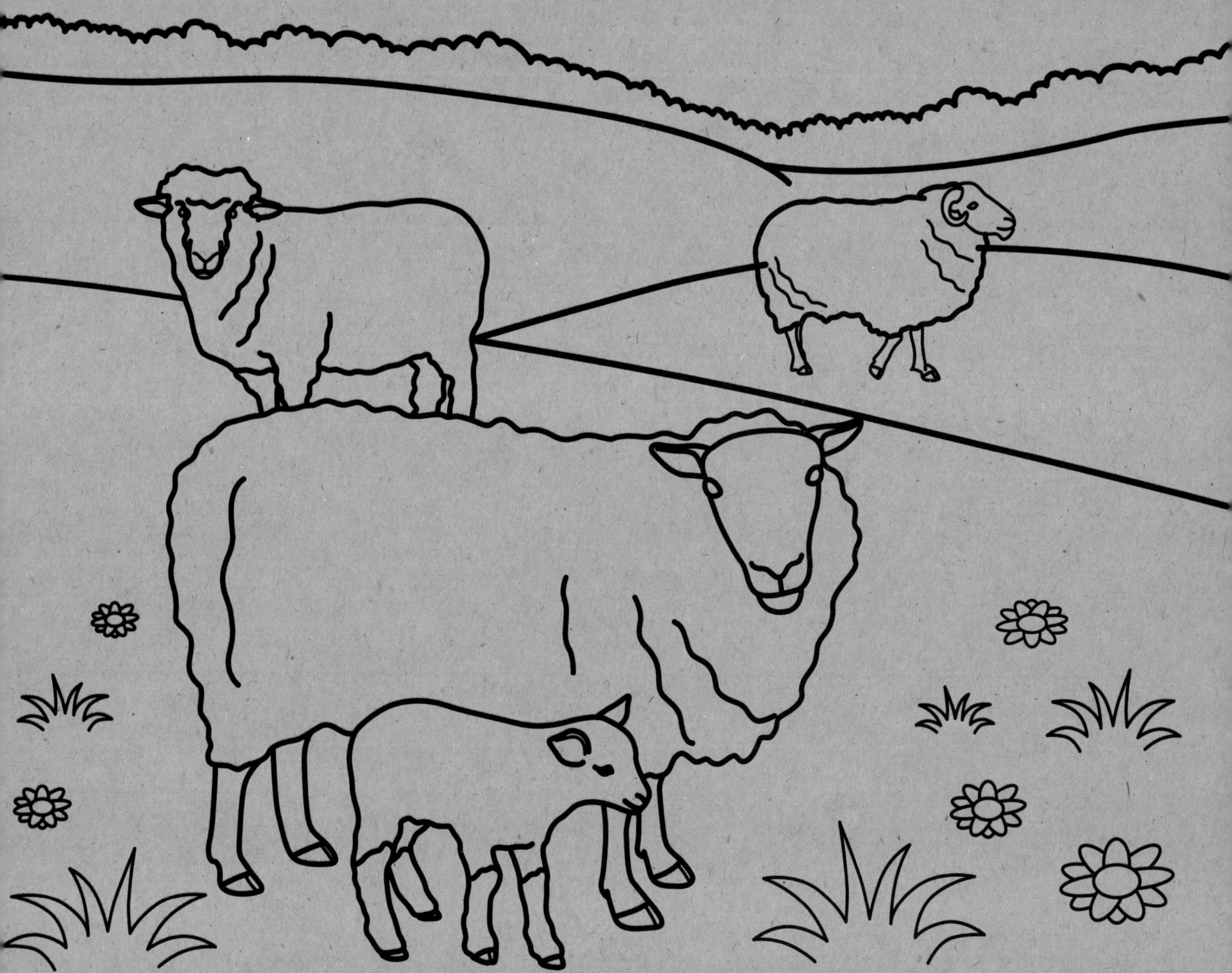

Letter practice

Trace over the outlines to practice writing letters.

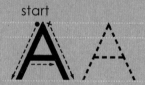 

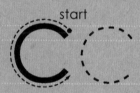 

 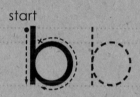

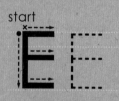 

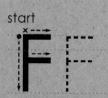

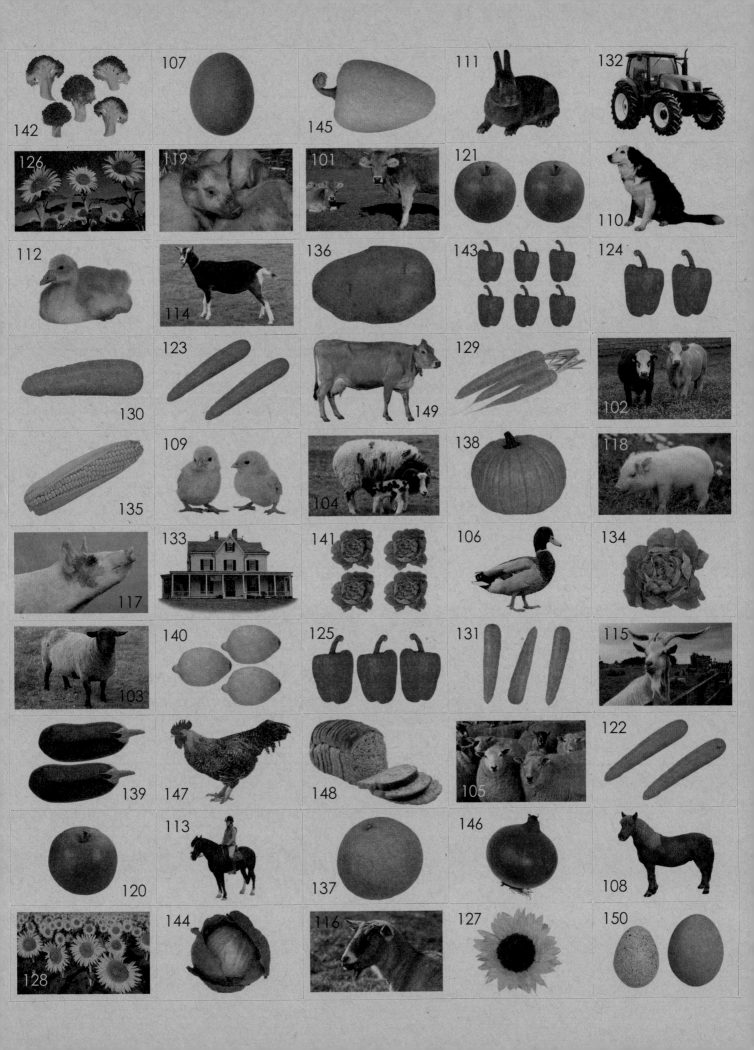

142

107

145

111

132

126

119

101

121

110

112

114

136

143

124

130

123

149

129

102

135

109

104

138

118

117

133

141

106

134

103

140

125

131

115

139

147

148

105

122

120

113

137

146

108

128

144

116

127

150

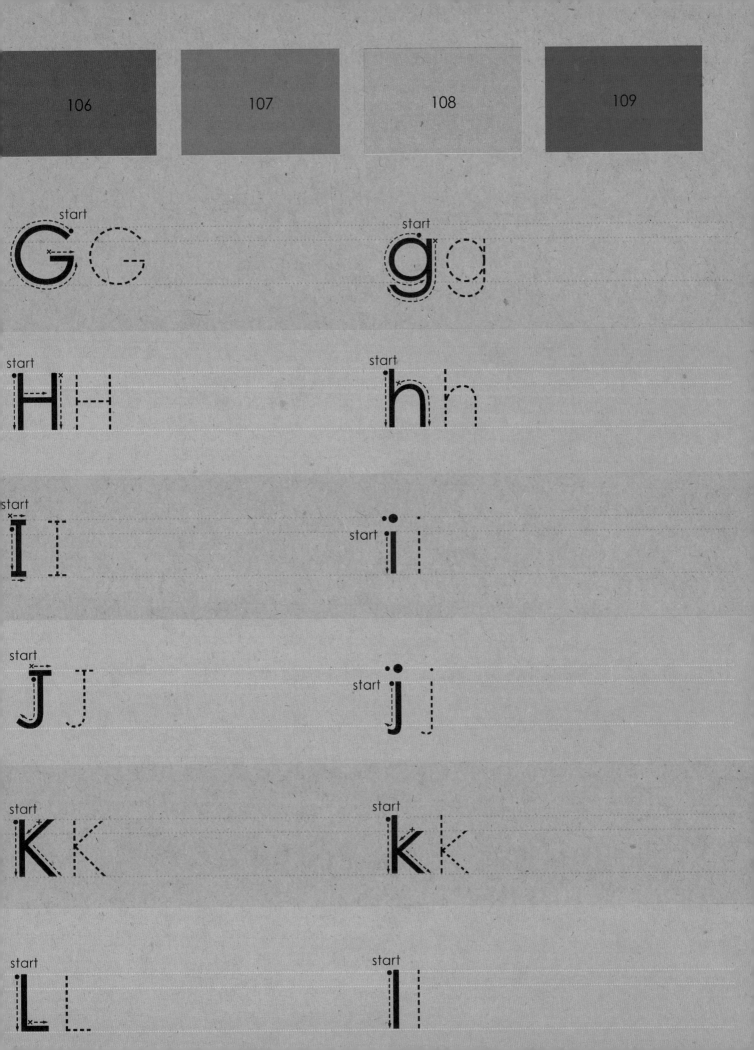

106 107 108 109

start G G

start g g

start H H

start h h

start I I

start i i

start J J

start j j

start K K

start k k

start L L

start l l

Letter practice

Trace over the outlines to practice writing letters.

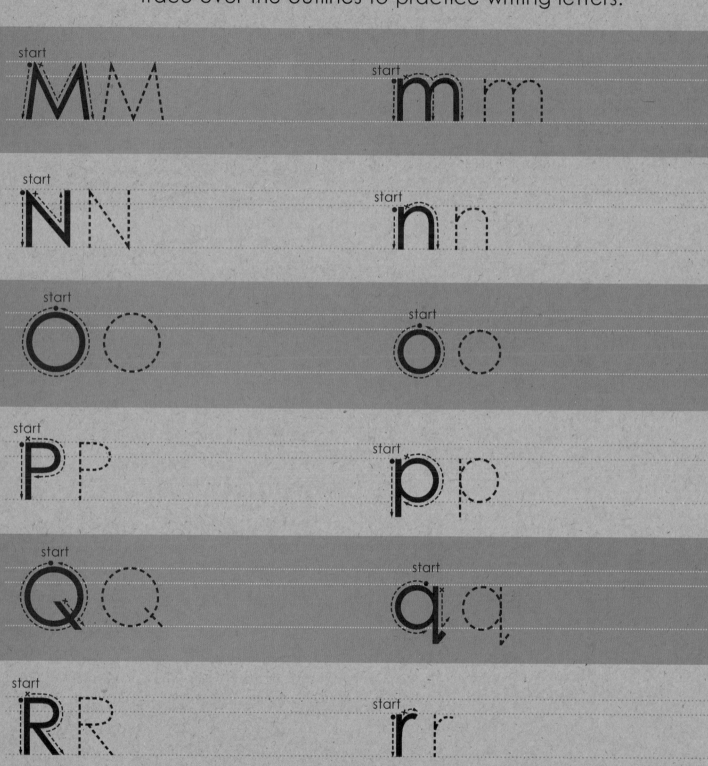

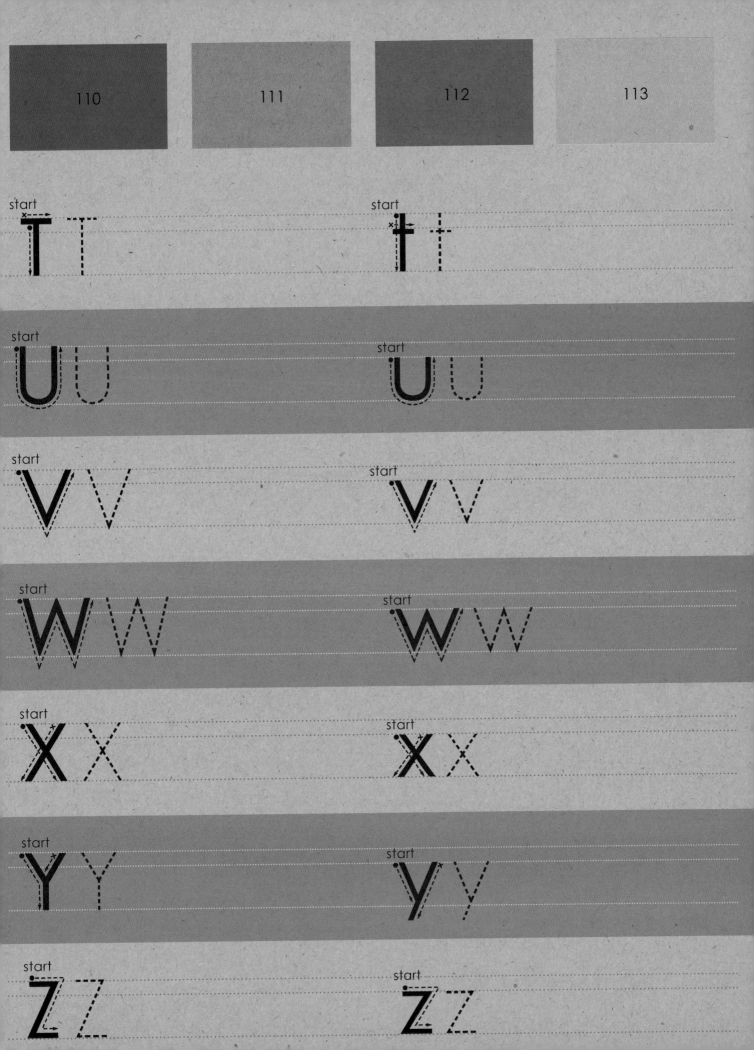

110   111   112   113

start
T T

start
t t

start
U U

start
U U

start
V V

start
V V

start
W W

start
W W

start
X X

start
X X

start
Y Y

start
Y Y

start
Z Z

start
Z Z

Goats and pig

Can you color in the animals to make this scene look really great?

114

115

116

Which animal has a curly tail?

117

118

119

An ORCHARD is where **apples** are found, Some on the trees and SOME on the ground

DO you LIKE to eat **cereal** for breakfast?

Farm fo

Bread
DO **you** have a favorite **SPREAD** to **put** on to your toast or **BREAD?**

PEAS GROW TOGETHER

Eating **LETTUCE** keeps YOU healthy!

Red or yellow, sour or sweet, **TOMATOES** grow best in the HEAT

ods

Which **potato** do you like the most? **Mashed** or baked, boiled or **roast?**

carrots
Rabbits LOVE to munch and **munch,** on carrots with their tasty **crunch**

wheat is GROUND into flour to make BREAD and **cakes**

a POD

Adding crops

Write the number of crops in the boxes, then add them up.

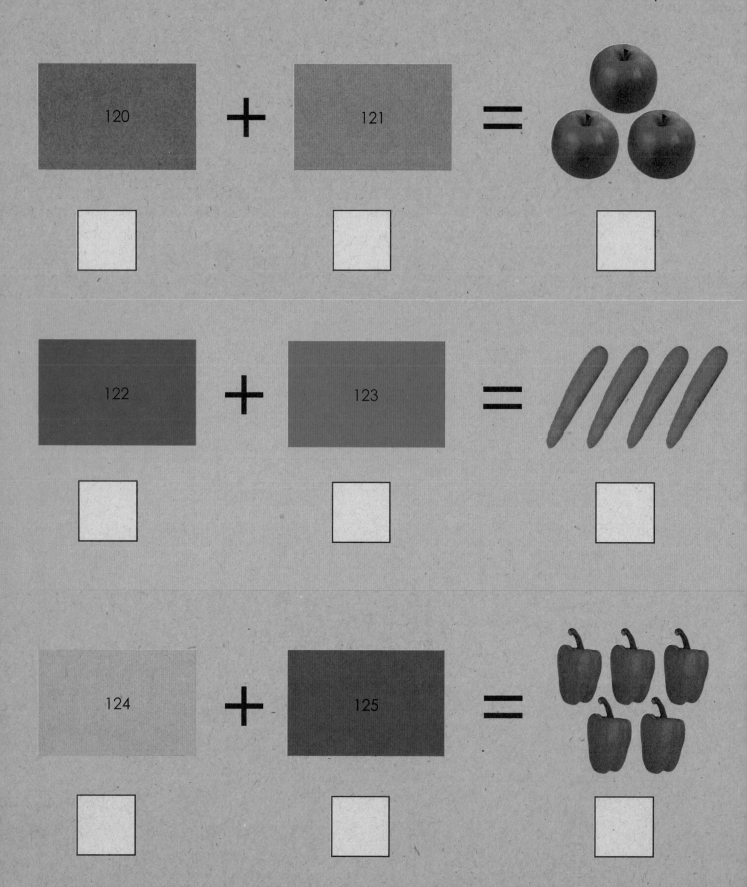

Pretty sunflowers

Color in the sunflowers, then trace over their name.

126

127

128

sunflowers

Crunchy carrots

Color in the carrots, then trace over their name.

129	130	131

carrots

Tractor maze

Can you find a way through the maze to lead the tractor to the farmhouse?

132

Start

Finish 133

Counting crops

Count the crops and write
the totals in the boxes.

How many
lettuces
can you
count?

How many
corn cobs
can you
count?

Coloring farm fruits

Can you color in the tasty farm fruits?

cherries

strawberry

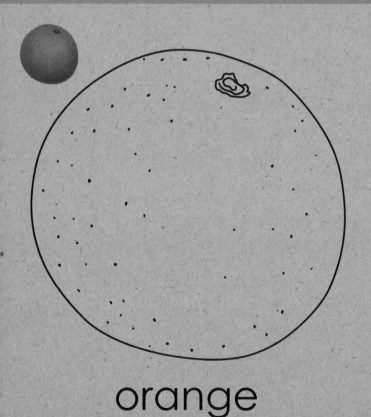

orange

bananas

Writing practice

Trace over the outlines to write the names of the farm vegetables.

onion

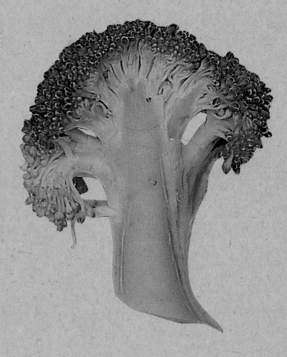

broccoli

carrots

pumpkin

Number practice

Trace over the outlines to practice writing numbers.

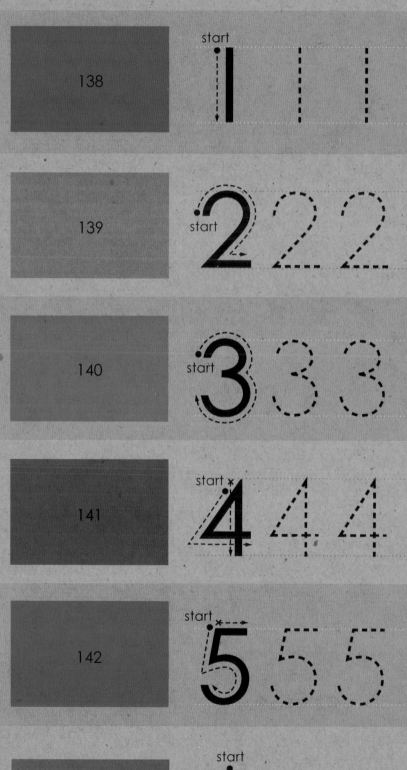

138

139

140

141

142

143

start
7 7 7

start
8 8 8

start
9 9 9

start start
10 10 10

start start
11 11 11

start
start
12 12 12

Mix and match

Can you draw lines between the farm animals and crops and the things we get from them?

147

148

149

150

151

152

153

154

Word search

Can you find the farm animals in the word search?

g	y	r	d	p	i	g	l	e	t
a	y	i	a	a	m	k	t	a	a
r	e	r	l	e	i	d	r	n	h
e	g	o	a	t	o	r	z	c	p
m	w	e	m	o	i	x	l	c	o
h	i	q	b	z	t	j	u	o	n
d	l	p	s	r	e	m	t	u	y
x	l	e	x	r	h	d	o	r	r
e	a	e	t	h	u	e	n	l	m
n	m	z	g	o	s	l	i	n	g
z	a	g	u	w	h	d	q	j	l
u	j	e	q	c	s	t	l	r	e

155
lamb

156
gosling

157
llama

158
goat

159
pony

160
piglet

Writing practice

Trace over the outlines to write the names of the animals.

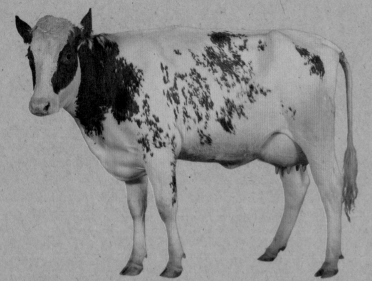

161

cow

ducklings

guinea pigs

162

sheepdog   chicks

Chicken trail

Which trail will lead the hen to her chicks?

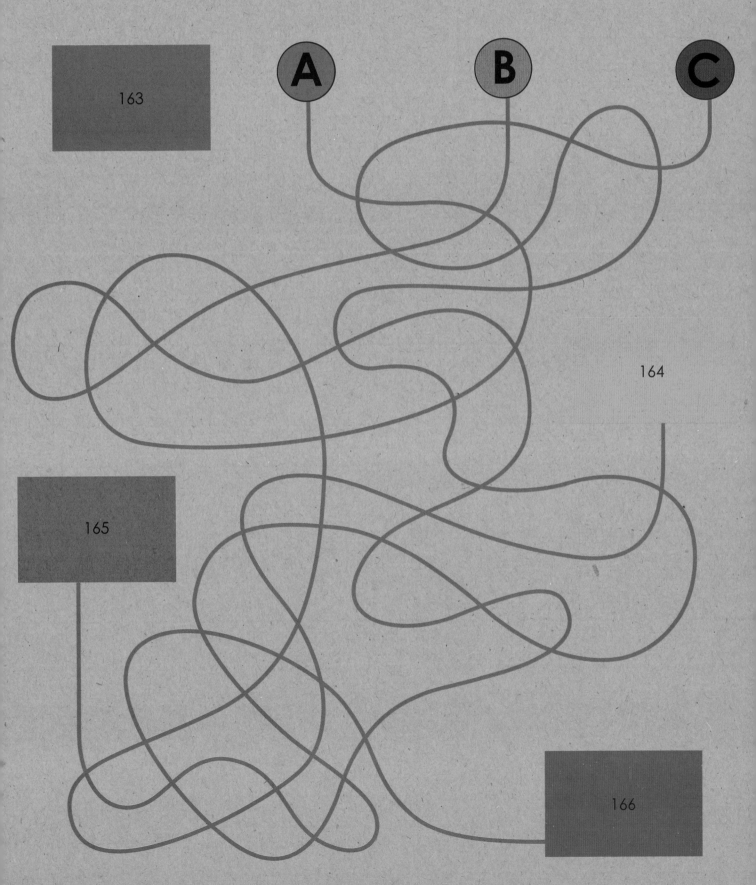

Who's missing?

Circle the farm animal that is in picture A, but is missing from picture B.

Friendly Sheepdog

Color in the sheepdog, then trace over its name.

167	168	169

sheepdog

Tractor

Painted red, blue or **GREEN**, it's everyone's **FAVORITE** farm machine

LIFTING and **SHIFTING** seed and grain, **FRONT LOADER** drives down the lane

Tracked tractor's

good when the going's **TOUGH**, it **travels** over ground so rough

The **baler** makes bales from hay,
for ANIMALS to eat all day

Busy machines

Telescopic forklift

Lifting up and down is
this **machine's** role,
it's a *ZIPPY* truck that's
tricky to CONTROL

Plowing the field

Can you color the tractor and plow to make this scene really colorful?

170

171

172

Have you ever seen a tractor?

173

174

175

What's different?

Can you spot six differences between these two pictures? Circle them on picture B.

A

B

How many?

Count the farm things and write the totals in the boxes.

 176

The **PLOW** turns over the soil so that seeds can be **PLANTED**

Machines at work

To **TEAR** around the farm at **speed**, a nippy **ATV** is what you **NEED**

Taking a HORSE to a race or show,
the **horsecar** is the way to go

This trailer carries sheep aplenty,
they travel in groups of more than 20!

Combine harvester

At harvest time
it never **stops**
it's when I must
collect the **crops!**

All-terrain vehicle

Color in the all-terrain vehicle, then trace over its name.

177	178	179

all-terrain vehicle

Who's missing?

Circle the farm machine that is in picture A, but is missing from picture B.

Friendly cows

Can you color in these different types of cows?

180	181	182

Highland

Jersey

183

184

185

Texas
longhorn

Friesian

Adding animals

Add the animals and write the numbers in the boxes.

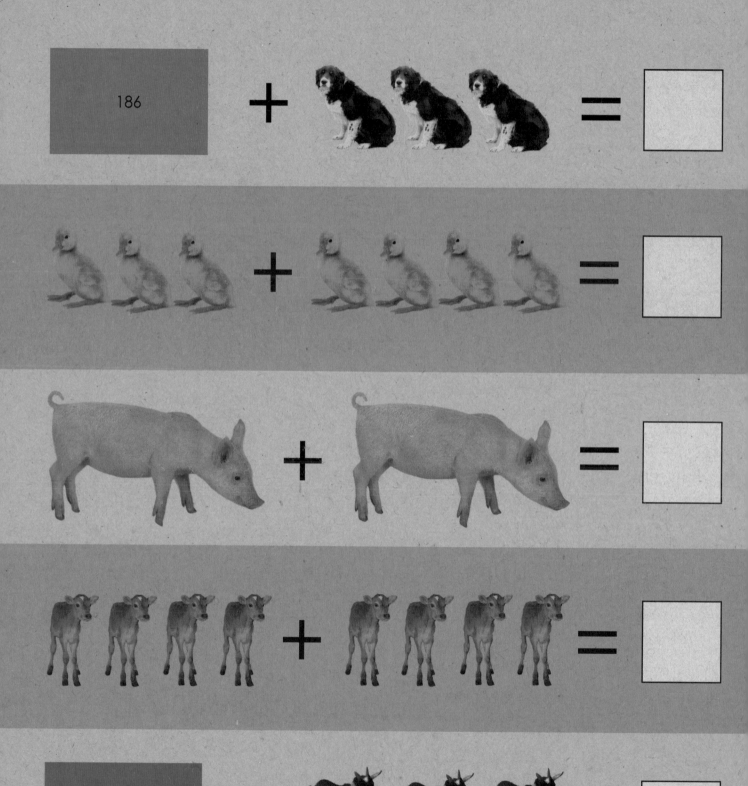

Hungry cow trail

Which trail will lead the cow to her feed?

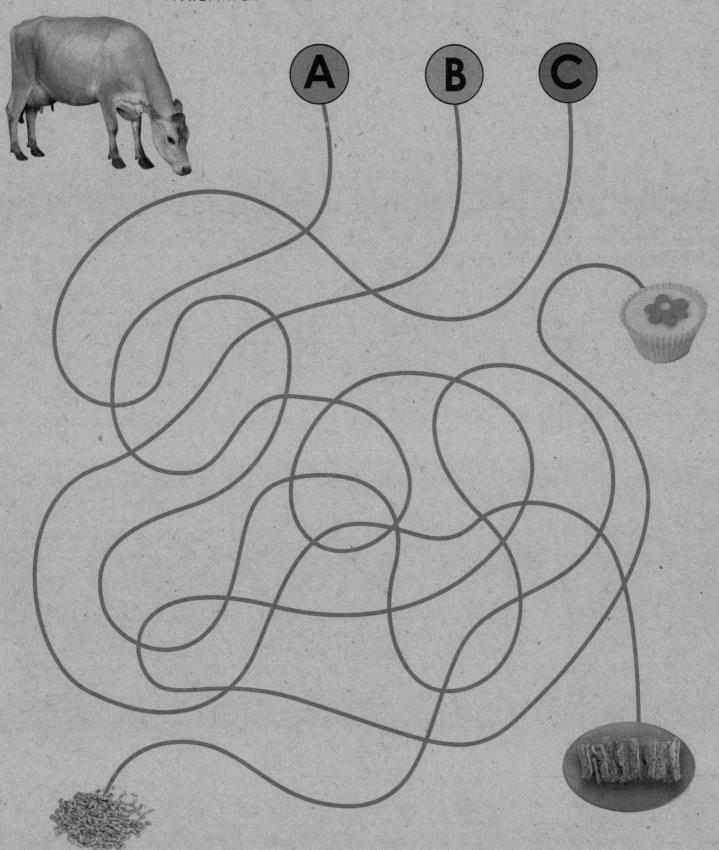

Odd ones out

Can you circle the chicks that are the wrong color?

Linking lines

Can you draw a line between each fruit and vegetable and the color it matches?

CHICKS
"cheep cheep"

TURKEY
"gobble gobble"

"meow"
CAT

Farm no

DONKEY
"ee-aw"

COW
"moo moo"

"baa baaa"
SHEEP

MOUSE
"squeak squeak"

PIG
"oink oink"

GOAT
"naa naaa"

"neigh"
HORSE

DUCK
"quack quack"

"honk honk"

GOOSE

ses

ROOSTER
"cock-a-doodle-doo"

"woof woof"

DOG

What's different?

Can you spot six differences between these two pictures? Circle them on picture B.

Word search

Can you find the farm things in the word search?

mouse

barn

rabbit

d	o	n	k	e	y	g	d	o	y
w	u	r	a	a	m	k	t	k	p
r	h	a	p	l	n	d	r	i	h
e	v	b	a	t	o	r	z	t	o
a	u	b	w	m	i	m	l	t	h
h	i	i	b	o	t	j	u	e	g
d	k	t	s	u	e	s	t	n	d
x	a	e	x	s	h	d	o	r	y
e	r	e	t	e	u	e	n	l	m
n	z	i	p	y	v	m	b	z	i
s	h	e	e	p	h	b	a	r	n
u	j	e	f	c	s	t	l	r	e

sheep

kitten

donkey

Barnyard Scene

Color in the barnyard scene. Which animal is eating grass?

188

189

190

pig

chickens

191

192

193

sheep

cow

Counting farm animals

Count the farm animals and write the totals in the boxes.

How many cows can you count?

194

How many pigs can you count?

195

How many
chickens can
you count?

How many
chicks can
you count?

How many
goats can
you count?

196

How many
horses can
you count?

197

Cute piglets

Color in the piglets, then trace over their name.

198   199   200

piglets